Celebrating Cultures

Buddha Day

Jill Foran

WEIGL PUBLISHERS INC.

Published by Weigl Publishers Inc.
123 South Broad Street, Box 227
Mankato, MN, 56002, USA
Web site: www.weigl.com

Library of Congress Cataloging-in-Publication Data

Foran, Jill.
   Buddha Day / by Jill Foran.
      p. cm.
   Summary: Discusses how the celebration of Wesak, or
Buddha Day, came about, what it signifies, and the ways in
which it is celebrated today.
   Includes bibliographical references and index.
   ISBN 1-59036-090-7 (Library Bound : alk. paper)
   1. Wesak--Juvenile literature. 2. Gautama Buddha--Juvenile
literature.   [1. Wesak. 2. Fasts and feasts--Buddhism.
3. Buddhism--Customs and practices. 4. Holidays. 5. Buddha.]
I. Title.
BQ5720.W4F67 2003
294.3'436--dc21

                                        2002014564

Printed in the United States of America
1 2 3 4 5 6 7 8 9 0 06 05 04 03 02

Project Coordinator Heather Kissock **Design & Layout** Bryan Pezzi
Copy Editor Jennifer Nault **Photo Researcher** Wendy Cosh

Photograph Credits

Every reasonable effort has been made to trace ownership and to obtain permission to reprint copyright material.
The publishers would be pleased to have any errors or omissions brought to their attention so that they may be
corrected in subsequent printings.

Cover: Golden Buddha Statues (Blair Redlin); **Corel Corporation:** pages 5, 8, 9, 10L, 10R, 11, 12T, 12B, 13B, 14,
15, 16, 17, 19R, 21; **MaXx Images:** page 7; **Katherine Phillips:** page 18; **Blair Redlin:** pages 3, 4, 22; **Janice
Redlin:** pages 6, 13T; ©Alison Wright/**CORBIS/MAGMA:** page 19L.

Contents

Happy Buddha Day!

Buddha helped people understand the meaning of life.

Every May, millions of people worldwide celebrate Buddha Day. This joyful event honors the birthday of the Buddha. *Buddha* means "**Enlightened** One." This name was given to a man who lived in India long ago. The man was very wise and kind. The Buddha was the **founder** of Buddhism. Today, Buddhism is one of the world's major religions. People who follow the teachings of Buddhism are called Buddhists.

Golden statues of Buddha are very common in the Buddhist religion.

Most Buddhists celebrate Buddha Day on the first day of the full Moon in May. It is believed that the Buddha was born on this day many years ago. For many Buddhists, Buddha Day is more than a birthday celebration. The celebration also honors the day that the Buddha became enlightened and the day that he died.

Vesak is another name for Buddha Day. In India, Vesak is the name of the month in which the Buddha was born.

INDIA

Monks are a common sight in Buddhist countries. These men promise to share the Buddha's teachings with others.

Becoming the Buddha

Siddhartha saw human suffering for the first time in his life.

The Buddha was born about 2,500 years ago. His parents were rulers of a kingdom in Northern India. They named their newborn son Siddhartha Gautama. Siddhartha's father did not want him to ever feel pain or sorrow. He hid Siddhartha away from the public in a palace. Siddhartha was an intelligent child. He studied many subjects. As time passed, Siddhartha grew curious about the outside world. He secretly left the palace to explore this outside world. Outside the palace, Siddhartha saw human suffering and death for the first time in his life. He could not understand why people had to suffer.

Buddha is honored in many ways, including artwork.

Later, at 29 years of age, Siddhartha left the palace in search of answers. He wanted to answer the important questions of life. How could humans make the world a better place? How could they find peace in their lives? He searched for answers to these questions for many years. One morning, Siddhartha sat under a **bodhi tree**. He decided that he would not move until he found the answers that he sought. He sat under the tree for a long time. Finally, Siddhartha reached Enlightenment. He discovered how people could find **inner peace**.

Siddhartha was 35 years old when he reached Enlightenment and became the Buddha.

Monks teach their students about Buddha's Enlightenment.

The Growth of Buddhism

The Buddha taught people how to find inner peace.

The Buddha was a generous man. He wanted to share his knowledge with other people. The Buddha spent the rest of his life teaching people how to find inner peace. He was surrounded by his loyal followers when he died at 80 years of age. After his death, his followers in India continued to honor the Buddha. They brought his teachings to other Asian countries.

Men learn how to become monks at a very young age.

People continued to honor the Buddha hundreds of years after he died. They made statues in his image. They built **temples** where the followers of the Buddha could honor him. They continued to tell others about his teachings and to celebrate his life. In the 1800s and early 1900s, many people from Asia began to move to the United States. They practiced their Buddhist beliefs in their new country.

There are many different types of Buddhism. Despite the differences in beliefs, all Buddhists honor the Buddha.

Buddhist temples can be found in many parts of the world.

Buddhists decorate their homes with flowers and flags.

Today, Buddhists throughout the world celebrate Buddha Day. Buddhists decorate their homes with flowers and Buddhist flags on this day. Many go to their local temple in the morning. Buddhists offer food to the monks who live at the temple. They also listen to special **sermons**. Later in the day, followers **chant** the Buddha's teachings and **meditate**.

Some monks play special instruments called long horns.

Buddhists often gather in groups to meditate.

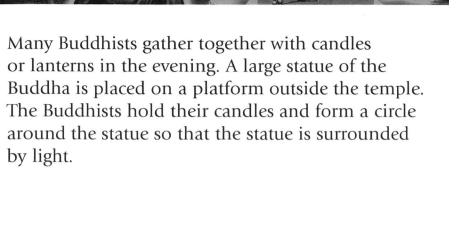

Many Buddhists gather together with candles or lanterns in the evening. A large statue of the Buddha is placed on a platform outside the temple. The Buddhists hold their candles and form a circle around the statue so that the statue is surrounded by light.

On Buddha Day, Japanese Buddhists pour sweet tea over a statue of the Buddha. This tradition comes from a legend that tells that the Buddha was bathed in pure water at birth.

Statues of the Buddha show him with his hands resting in his lap. This pose represents peace and love to Buddhists.

Americans Celebrate

Buddhists across the United States celebrate Buddha Day. They hold large, public ceremonies to honor the Buddha. Most of the ceremonies are open to people who are not Buddhist. This helps others learn about the Buddha and his teachings. Following are just a few of the places in the United States that celebrate Buddha Day.

On Buddha Day, beautiful ceremonies take place all over Hawai'i. Offerings of tropical flowers are placed at the **altars** of Buddhist temples. Dances and flower shows are held for everyone to enjoy.

The Japanese American National Museum in Los Angeles, California, celebrates Buddha Day. The events include speeches on Buddhism, a flower festival, storytelling, and crafts for children.

Los Angeles

Hawai'i

In Chicago, Illinois, Buddha's birthday celebration lasts one weekend in May. It begins on Saturday with the Peace and Happiness Parade. Later in the day, people listen to sermons about Buddhism. Then, they enjoy a **vegetarian** feast. On Sunday, crowds gather to meditate, light lanterns, and chant.

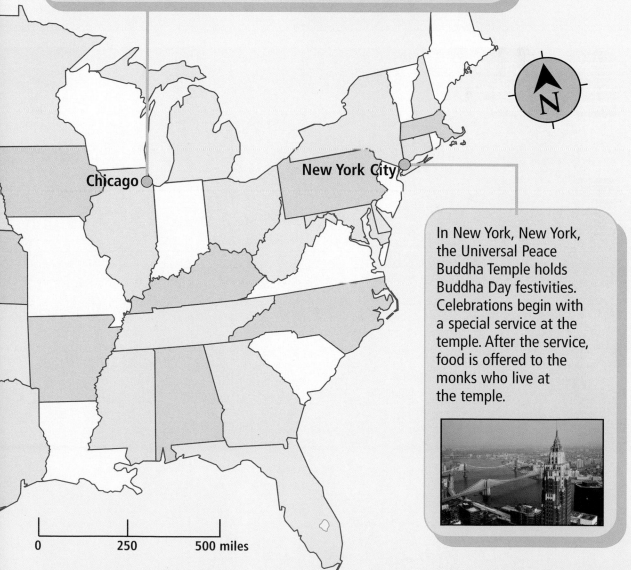

Chicago

New York City

N

In New York, New York, the Universal Peace Buddha Temple holds Buddha Day festivities. Celebrations begin with a special service at the temple. After the service, food is offered to the monks who live at the temple.

0   250   500 miles

Honoring the Buddha

Statues remind people of the Buddha's wisdom.

Statues of the Buddha

A statue of the Buddha is on display in a **shrine** during Buddha Day. To honor the day of his birth, this statue shows the Buddha as a newborn or young boy. For more than 2,000 years, Buddhists around the world have made statues of the Buddha. These statues serve to remind people of the Buddha's perfect **wisdom**. Buddhists try to develop this wisdom.

In many temples, the statue of the Buddha is placed in a central room. It is surrounded by other statues.

Meditation and Chanting

Many Buddhists meditate on Buddha Day. They think about the good qualities of the Buddha when they meditate. Buddhists believe that meditation helps to calm and focus the mind. Through meditation, some Buddhists are able to find peace and understanding. People also chant at Buddha Day ceremonies. Buddhists chant the teachings of the Buddha over and over. This helps them learn the Buddha's words.

At some Buddha Day ceremonies, scented water is poured over a statue of the Buddha. This reminds Buddhists to practice the Buddha's teachings so that their minds may be pure.

Buddhist nuns sometimes gather together to meditate. A nun is a woman who has promised to live by her religion's teachings.

Candles and Decorations

Buddhist children make special lanterns for Buddha Day.

Lights of Wisdom

On Buddha Day, Buddhists everywhere light candles or lanterns. Lit candles and lanterns represent wisdom. Many followers recall how Buddha became enlightened when a candle is lit. Buddhist children often make special lanterns for Buddha Day. They decorate their lanterns with objects that represent the Buddha's birth. Some people dedicate their lanterns to loved ones during Buddha Day ceremonies.

Lanterns are a popular decoration on Buddha Day. Lit lanterns represent the Enlightenment of Buddha.

Flowers for Buddha

Buddhists make **offerings** of flowers at Buddha Day ceremonies. Flowers decorate homes and temples. They serve to remind people of the Buddha's birth. According to legend, the Buddha was born in a beautiful garden. Flowers also remind people of the Buddha's teachings. The Buddha taught his followers that nothing in the world is permanent. Flowers are fresh and beautiful in the morning. As time passes, their beauty fades away.

The most common flower seen in Buddhist temples is the lotus. The lotus represents Enlightenment.

The lotus flower is holy in Buddhism because it rises out of the dark mud to become a bright bloom.

The Buddhist flag represents oneness among Buddhists.

A Colorful Flag

The Buddhist flag is hung during Buddha Day celebrations. This special flag is a symbol of **oneness** among all Buddhists. The flag has five vertical stripes and five horizontal stripes. The stripes are blue, yellow, red, white, and orange. Many Buddhists believe that these colors shone around the Buddha's head after he became enlightened.

The Buddhist flag was first flown in Sri Lanka in 1885.

A Special Tree

The bodhi tree is very important in Buddhism. This is because the Buddha became enlightened while sitting under a bodhi tree. Today, bodhi trees are found in Buddhist temples around the world. On Buddha Day, bodhi trees are decorated with flags and lanterns. Some Buddhists paint pictures on the leaves of bodhi trees. The leaves are given to others as gifts on Buddha Day.

Incense is often burned in honor of the Buddha. The sweet smell of burning incense serves to remind Buddhists to be pure and good.

Monks often gather under bodhi trees to meditate and pray.

For More Information

Many books and Web sites explain the history and traditions of Buddhism. To learn more about Buddhism and Buddha Day, you can borrow books from a library or search the Internet.

Books

The history of Buddhism and the Buddha can be explored by reading the following books.

Carew-Miller, Anna. *Buddha*. Broomall, Pennsylvania: Mason Crest Publishers, 2003.

Ries, Julien. *The Many Faces of Buddhism*. Broomall, Pennsylvania: Chelsea House Publishers, 2000.

Web Sites

For stories and drawings about Buddhism and the Buddha, visit **Gakkai Online** at: www.gakkaionline.net/kids

Enter the search words "Buddha" or "Buddhist" into an online encyclopedia, such as **Encarta** to learn more about this culture. www.encarta.com

Imagine if...

Buddhists around the world love to celebrate Buddha Day. They light candles, decorate their homes and temples, and meditate. This is a special day because it honors a very important man. Imagine that you are attending a Buddha Day celebration. What kinds of activities and events would you see? Write a story or draw a picture showing all of the things that you would see and do at the Buddha Day celebration.

What You Have Learned

1 Buddha Day celebrates the birthday of the Buddha. It also honors the Buddha's Enlightenment and his death.

2 The Buddha was born about 2,500 years ago. His name was Siddhartha Gautama.

3 The Buddha found truth and Enlightenment under the bodhi tree.

4 Asian people brought Buddhism to the United States in the 1800s and early 1900s.

5 Buddhists all over the world celebrate Buddha Day. They light candles, chant, and meditate.

6 Buddha Day is also known as Vesak.

More Facts to Know

- Some Buddhists celebrate Buddha Day in April instead of May.

- The Buddha's teachings are known as the *Dharma*. Buddhists believe that the Dharma is the guide to Enlightenment and truth.

- Buddhists believe that anyone can become enlightened. Everyone has the ability to become a Buddha.

- The Buddha spent 45 years teaching his followers about the truths that he discovered under the bodhi tree.

Words to Know

altars: holy tables or stands

bodhi tree: a tree found in India

chant: to sing certain words over and over

enlightened: to have gained complete understanding

founder: a person who begins a new religion

incense: a substance burned for its sweet smell

inner peace: calmness and happiness

meditate: to think deeply

offerings: objects given in ceremonies

oneness: agreement in mind, feeling, or purpose

pure: clean

sermons: religious talks or speeches

shrine: a structure or place devoted to a special person or god

temples: buildings where people go to pray

vegetarian: a person who does not eat meat

wisdom: knowledge based on experience

Index

4.6/.5